A Box
of
Crazy
Toys

100 Liquid Landscapes
by Peter Dellolio

XENOS BOOKS
IN COLLABORATION WITH
CHELSEA EDITIONS

ISBN 10: 1-879378-93-0
ISBN 13: 9781879378933

Cover art: *He Just Stood There Grinning* by Barbara Rachko.

This book was made possible by a grant from
the Raiziss-Giop Charitable Foundation.

Manufactured in the United States of America
by Thomson-Shore, Inc.

Xenos Books
Box 16433
Las Cruces, NM 88004
www.xenosbooks.com

Contents

Preface

THE POETRY in *A Box of Crazy Toys*, to quote the speakers from *The Clown's Three Large Buttons*, "pushes the boundaries of natural reality into an irrational realm . . . that is the purpose of such language when words are tossed about like a bunch of juggler's pins."

I have tried to give the reader a meal of different meanings, to alter the ingredients of the recipes, to grow the vegetables in some exotic, rich and strange soil. I wanted to transform language and the business of words into millions of gigantic movie screens attached like endless tapestries and illuminated by all the dreaming brains in the world.

I have always been excited by the challenge of harnessing the incantatory and exotic properties of language the way a surrealist painter manipulates paint, turning the canvas into a window on our subconscious, our fantasies and our dreams.

Language, especially poetry, gives the imagination the upper hand because words allow us to see the invisible, the irrational, the bizarre and the impossible. I hope these poems give the reader a pleasurable glimpse into the surreal world, with magic, abandon, innocence and the pure fun of words.

PETER DELLOLIO
Brooklyn, New York
November 1, 2017

A BOX OF CRAZY TOYS

For my parents
Marie & Pete

"A man can control only what he comprehends, and comprehend only what he is able to put into words . . . "

"But these words have no meaning!"

"At the moment, no, but they will. Or rather they may eventually acquire meaning . . . "

—Stanislaw Lem, *The Futurological Congress*

Skeleton Accordions

Skeleton accordions
play for the ocean.
Clown waves cough
up alabaster trunks
of white and green. A
tunnel of cake is encrusted
with radioactive pustules.
Silent films are
projected upon the
foreheads of children.
The little ones vomit
miniature skyscrapers made
of exotic African woods. Tonight
there is violence in
the cobalt mansion.

Children with Violin Faces

Children with violin faces
hover above deep wooden
soup bowls. Not steam but
clusters of arguing mosquitoes
emanate from the boiling
broth. Dressed in tight red
rubber Dutch clothing, the
boys and girls make
hammers out of the pasture
memories of a jade dog.

Droplets of Blood

A tiger with red clarinets
for legs is confused by
droplets of blood. One hundred transcripts
of the interrogation of a metal
rug, bound in cheeses of the world,
are being delivered to the
surgeon's house. The blood
followed him home, to murder
him no doubt, while the tiger,
hypnotized by a spider radio,
plays a riff in four octaves from *Sing Sing Sing*.

The Infant's Fingers

The infant's fingers are
fat thick fish. The
inflation of the digits is
colorful. Plenty of orange
red and green. Airborne
infant floating fish.

Meat Fires Writhe Musically

Meat fires writhe
musically inside an elevator,
hallucinating on narcotics.
The cockpit is overrun with
thousands of red ants. Tomorrow
the hunter will make a
peace treaty with his
collection of anger masks.

Propellers Made of Sparrows

Propellers made of sparrows
spin out of control during
the performance of a morbid
nocturne. Coffee incense burns
in the veiny red and lavender
trumpet. Yet the saliva
avalanche cannot prevent
the shuffling madmen
from disassembling the hallway.

He Was Attacked

He was attacked by a chaotic cluster
of geometrical shapes. The
ocean found a trigonometry
book and, after a long night
of opium, pretended to be
trapezoids and pentagons.

The Spindly Branches

The spindly branches,
winter-bare, are ebony
chocolates driven insane
by the cold. Dreaming
of desserts in warm German
pastry shops, they float
above the checkered ceramic
bistro tables.

Sulfur Mask

Sulfur mask on the
boxing chickens. Rope
the lamb into a very
lewd position. Thick
rectangular and dense
the Frankenstein head
of the pork chunk.
Deranged animals not
the farm Orwell planned.
Drugged farmers dreaming.

A Robe of Blue Silk

A robe of blue silk
demanded sex from the
coral scarecrow. Nothingness
wanted stale coffee
and fly mummies. Mud
revolvers spit urine into
the insane asylum.

Nightmare Premiere

Nightmare premiere of a
film noir feature in a palatial
1940s theater. Child leper
corpses in every seat. They
all wear detective trench coats
and whipped cream fedoras.
Linoleum masquerades in a
pewter tuxedo. The Egyptian
magician makes daffodil
maneuvers. Blood clots
have been sculpted into a
Communist toilet. No one
is laughing in the orange
gymnasium.

Ruby Fornicators

Ruby fornicators with
elaborate rashes on
their granite buttocks are
negotiating in the orchestra
pit with renegade black
and white Christmas balls.

A Cow Disguised as Einstein

A cow disguised as Einstein,
hung from its hooves,
is being delightfully whipped
in the Taj Mahal. The
echoes of leather
striking bovine flesh float
into an Irish bar
in lower Manhattan. Foam
on Moran's tankard vibrates
slightly.

Insect Jury

Insect jury. Implacable and
remote. Judge's bench made
from frozen sailor shirts.
The Defendant is a refrigerator
dressed in urine-soaked clown clothes.
The air in the courtroom gave
a transfusion to hand painted
vintage neck ties.

The Marbling of the Meat

The marbling of the meat
floor caused the caps of
the Pullman car operators to
turn the hexagonal liquid
knobs of the radio until
a fatalistic string quartet
by *Shostakovitch* was
found. This evoked
the sadness of children who,
having finished their replicas of
the guillotine used to execute
Marie Antoinette,
must be put to bed.

An Army of Turtle Doorknobs

An army of turtle doorknobs
launched an attack upon the
palsy-ridden construction site.
Involuntarily shaking beams
and platforms, trying to
dance with lavender bagpipes
coated with green Vaseline, were
no match for the turtles,
expertly commanded by a
gecko General wearing a toolbox
turban.

A Glass Chest of Drawers

A glass chest of drawers,
filled with tropical fish,
on a Mexican shore.
Cornucopia of darting
colors shining under the
fruit-rich rays of the
Cancun sun. The
furniture mover, turned
into brass, reaches in
vain for the bureau knobs
where a few
rainbow Tetras flit by.
His sweat rag, unfurled
in a permanent metal
loop, droops over his
back pocket.

Silvery Sombrero Breakfast

A silvery sombrero breakfast
investigates a circular
flapping diary sandwich while
windowsill smell boats speak
Pig Latin to androgynous
spider milkshakes.

Ocean Bandage

Ocean
      bandage
          burst hate
      manure symphony shouting
      vegetables
      perfume
      desks
      smell of love
          always.

Smiling Tubas

Smiling Tubas have
decided that the pasta
was over cooked. Nude Chef
has infected muscle thoughts.
Conveyor belt moves in
slow motion, transporting
blind kittens in white
lab coats.

Slab of Hypnotized Bubbles

Slab of hypnotized bubbles
organizes a committee of
test tubes for the purpose
of protesting against a
pyramidal box of jester
candy. One of the bubbles,
an Anarchist with an
advanced thyroid condition,
sings an aria from
La Traviata.

Cooked Shadows Pretend

Cooked shadows pretend
that the beetle's neck
is made of rose paste.
The auditorium is filled
with thousands of cacti
in glowing infection costumes.
Brittle bamboo fences
rattling in the wind
clack like oyster castanets.

Dead Soup Lather

Dead soup lather under
attack. Sausage shoes being
overcharged for magnesium
dummy sex. Fragrant
android apron puts a fresh
canvas on the marble easel.

Iodine Gems

Iodine gems wrestle
inside the throat of a
narcoleptic maestro. The tuna
staircase plays an oboe covered
with hysterical maggots. An
elephant with obsessive-compulsive
disorder, wearing a hand-stitched
leather S & M costume, is driving
a pink trolley towards a
bordello made of orange and
lime-green stone.

Pirates Playing Piccolos

Pirates playing piccolos made
of corn have demanded a
review of the cheese bricks
from the *Alamo* explosion.
Saint Francis of Assisi
has intervened. A
battalion of Peruvian enema
bags swaps drunken
stories with magnetic pus birds.

A Bucket

A bucket filled with
zebra stripes and pearl
syringes translated every issue
of *TV Guide* into
Aramaic. Luckily, all of the
rectangular oatmeal rooms, populated
with stumbling faceless professors
wearing raincoats made of
duck eyes, treated the buckets
with tenderness and respect.
A talcum powder statue
played the bassoon, nodding in
approval.

The Balcony Wanted to Taste

The balcony wanted to taste
the wooden circulatory system.
French desserts, made of
tarantula parts and diced
derbies, hobbled toward the
sexy staircase. Imagine the
balcony's surprise when
thousands of *Play-Doh* spinal cords
regurgitated war
bonds posters!

The Little Boy

The little boy, wearing
safari-cursed, brittle pants,
danced for the pond
water briefcase. A red
pen followed him. A
disturbed vegetal mandolin
had eczema.

An Ambassadorial Syringe

An ambassadorial syringe,
armed with concrete hinges
and coquettish swings,
startled the nutmeg-nuanced,
perfectly turned wooden
chess pieces, while the
Abbey sluggishly climbed
the mountain.

The String Quartet

Inside the
pastel embalming
room, Mexican
midgets, having formed
a felicitous firing squad,
twitch and wiggle
with sultry sensuality
while a string
quartet plays a
haunting melody
in D minor.

A Rubber Floor

A rubber floor asked
to be forgiven. Pink
plates went on a pilgrimage.
Nude thoughts ate an algebraic
breakfast during a
slapstick version of
The Crucifixion.

Mumbling Zinc Headaches

Mumbling zinc headaches
made the lascivious blue prints
do an alkaline tool dance
while the lavender scaffold
played a jeweled harp in
the orange moonlight.

Emerald Balloon Shadows

Emerald balloon shadows
smell like red hots from
the ninth inning of a
Murderer's Row game. Stingy
Aztec robots play colonic
solitaire with vinyl cardinal
skullcaps. Lorenzo the
Asperger's Syndrome weight lifter sniffs
the air on the toasted deck
of an infant ship.

Maggot Wheels

Maggot wheels on
the sirloin roller coaster.
Cream puff nipples on
the muscular breast
of the lion tamer.
All chaos within the
morphine-drenched carnival,
spinning under a
barnacle-encrusted sun.

Mesmerized Kite Canvas

Mesmerized kite canvas drenched in
red lotion, arguing vehemently with
candid skull fans in a pink hatred desert,
reveals at the last moment that its
collection of snaky coal vests was
stolen from a brilliant bronze bulldozer.

Regions of the World

Etched upon the clown-globe
in wild contours of grease paint,
the majestic regions of the world
invite a classroom of children
to wonder
with thrilled eyes
about the multi-layered
adventures of planet Earth.
Holding peanut butter pencils
between red alligator fingers,
the boys and girls have
equatorial longings.

Wooden Raindrops

Wooden raindrops
in a tumultuous storm
accumulate rapidly, forming
a slaughter-house where
zebras in yellow space
costumes strip sows
of their succulent flesh
and a somnambulant
jeep peacefully asleep dreams
of the meaty feet of
an escaping yak.

Card Trick

Card trick on the
pink mattress
floating across the ocean.

Raped Hats Emit Farts

Raped hats emit farts
of ancient Chinese
flute music. Pugilistic
window thoughts do
not want to ride
the elevator because
goat whistles are
covered in slippery
warm blood. Tank
tasks tonight. No
time for tight rope
tapestries.

Screaming Walls

Screaming walls
infused with dreams
of boats. The
boat barnacles are
bulbous and hard.
The walls are
covered with pink
silk wallpaper
which flaps from
the screams moving
the air.

The Waves Rise and Curl Forward

The waves rise and curl forward
as they turn into thousands of
onyx chessboards. Under the
transformative glare of the beating
sun, the board squares swirl,
mixing together, as if they were
seawater, cascading color cadences
of green pink blue. Little units
of ocean and the dignified
seriousness of chess.

Night Watchman

The circular body of the
banjo, creamy white and taut,
has transformed into a glowering
metal pumpkin during the
night watchman's nightmare.
He tried to play it, to serenade
an assembly of undertakers with
dragonflies for eyes, but the
evil orange mouth kept biting
off his fingers. One by one,
the bloody digits took the stage
and performed a particularly lewd
version of a *Can-Can*. The
sexuality of the atmosphere was
intense. In the last row of the
hall, adding to the autumnal ingredient
and summoning some of the playful
horror of Halloween, two scarecrows
made of gambling dice flipped and
rolled in a fornicating frenzy.

Tumbleweed Milky

Tumbleweed milky and
hat, are you serious?
Lately I have been in lard.
How are the veins?
Strongbox Joe eats barbells
made of trout pâté.
Eyeballs and ladders found me.
Dental disfigurement said,
Where is my foot?
Trapdoors in the teak steps
slide open to reveal atomic blast
dummies playing Bach trumpets.

Larry said, *A wretch like me.*

Flavor Tundra

Flavor tundra specious
blanket wizard
on a frame from
Strangers on a Train
Farley's tuna special
on the sexual Merry-Go-Round.

Rented Magnet Trucks

Rented magnet trucks have
made bullions of water. The
insidious gray passageways of
1950s Science Fiction films
contain angular shadows and
limp rubber monster costumes
lying on the floor. *Captain
Rocket*, a muscular manly
crew cut space hero, is eating
a titanium memory omelet
while he studies a diorama
of bizarre cavemen sexual
rituals. The Neanderthal
cave camp has many small
fires burning. Flash images
of *Van Gogh*'s sunflowers
appear in the orange
and yellow flame forms.

Suddenly, the compartment door
to the Captain's quarters
slides open with a strange
deep space hiss.

Someone with Little Lizards

Someone with little lizards
for eyes insulted the mud
center of a square nectarine.
This attracted the attention
of the circles and triangles
in the tubercular architect's
drafting tool. Suddenly, the
hundreds of crumpled, blood stained
tissues (used by the architect
to collect his slimy cough
phlegm) began a slow motion
performance of *The Blue Danube*.
At that moment a stagehand,
standing high up on a rafter
beam, held a blowtorch to
his head, causing it to quickly melt.
Gray rivulets of clay. Pipe
cleaners revealed. No skull.
The lizards spun around in
the impolite gentleman's sockets,
excited by the excellent dancing.

Elmer Season

Tendon soup vases were
overwhelmed with pencil-thin
sexual manuals. An inordinately
robust avocado, proudly preening
its bulging almost mousse-like
green flesh, entered the room
wearing an authentic *Flying
Aces* World War II bomber jacket.
Maurice the dapper spy
chuckled. The film snapped
just as *Bugs* and *Daffy*
ripped the last poster off
the tree. Flickering shadows
and eerie projector beams
danced across the surface:
Elmer Season.

Harpo's Raincoat

The bicycle, bereft of horn,
is simply overcome with riotous laughter.
Even though the bulbous red honker
protrudes from Harpo's mischievously
disheveled raincoat, how could
this two-wheeled (bespoken!)
machine, wandering willy-nilly
after the comedian's theft, become
angry at such
innocent chicanery? Perhaps to sympathize
with the bicycle's reliance on the sound of its horn,
Harpo plays his harp. Now bicycle and
Marx brother shed glistening
tears in which overlapping images of a mustard brown
spider appear. The insect glides across the web,
and in its charming pantomime
of Harpo's angelic glissandi,
makes sweet silent music of its own.

The Clown's Three Large Buttons

The clown's three large
buttons are pink snowball
cakes. A black hole of
sugar and cream filling.
Drill Sergeant with red
metal eyebrows checks off
his requirements on a
laser beam clipboard. He
insults the clown with
barking dog pencil heads
and a trunk full of
Eat at Joe's signs made
of neon insects. An It!
The Terror from Beyond Space
rocket ship emerges with
a kind of chocolate verticality
from the gravity clutches of
the foamy collapsed star buttons.
In a long series of rectangular
windows, the relieved faces of the
crew can be seen. They smile
sardonically at the Sergeant's
eyebrows because the metal used
to make them was delivered
in a monkey crate coated with

fear slime from a dolphin's
nightmare. The fish, part
of a limestone totem pole, attracted
special attention because it alone
was carved from a solid block
of cherry wood. The notion
that the pink buttons and
the cherry wood have a kind
of aesthetic candy-cake relationship
is purely a product of analogy
and the crewmembers shake
their heads, believing that this sort
of gestalt or perceptual symbiosis
pushes the boundaries of
natural reality into an irrational
realm. "But that is the purpose
of such language when words are
tossed about like a bunch of juggler's
pins," shouts the clown through a
large bullhorn made of polka dot
tuna flesh. The dolphin, weeping
for its fallen brethren, slaughtered
and fashioned into this artificial
speaking device, dons a whipped cream
space helmet and floats towards the
rocket.

Conundrum Tom-Tom

Conundrum
tom-tom is
a pink rubber
bon-bon in
a straw case.

It's a candy
store
gored by the icicle
horn of a horny
unicorn.

Elevator men in
corn tuxedos pull
the lift levers
with torn tobacco
fingers.

The ennui lingers
and gingerly the
talcum powder triggers
separate from the
handsome revolvers.

Lobster Puppets

Lobster puppets nervously flip
the leather pages of an Egyptian
road map.

Wearing a 1901 driving costume,
including goggles and gloves, the
mummified chef mentally reviews
his revolving recipes.

The Slick Wet Skin

The slick wet skin of
the morning-bright yellow
fireman's raincoat is having
a philosophical debate with
a four-drawer machine age
filing cabinet from the 1930s.
There are lewd color 8x10
photos of metal penguins in
the second drawer from the
bottom. The top drawer is
crammed with domino-sized liver
tablets engraved with oyster jam impressions
of *Sir Isaac Newton.*

Ebony Bassoon Flesh

Ebony bassoon flesh infested
with maggots wearing turbans
they pinch their way in and out
of the black tube of tissue
like anthrax specimens on a
slide in a biohazard lab
where a tall muscular manly
lesbian has secured a *Tumblelina*
doll to an exam table made of
eggshells and Eskimo stomachs
the exam room is a gigantic
fish tank glass walls reveal
giant turtles swimming in menstrual
blood wearing *Howdy Doody*
masks so you can see why I
decided to play the ukulele
even though my fingers are
frozen parrots who were *New
Dealers* and campaigned for *FDR*
on the promise of a steak dinner.

Let's Go with the Idea

Let's go with the idea that present
past and future are like a strip of
celluloid it is always there always unfurling
so Caruso is still singing two hundred
feet back and your baby is using a
walker three hundred feet forward the film
like time and space has no finite line
of demarcation now W. C. Fields' juggling
pins spin in the glare of the movie lights
while the opening chord of *A Hard Day's Night*
resonates under the shell of the Hollywood
Bowl and the intoxicating aromas of all the
Salumerias in 1914 Little Italy mesmerize
the senses even though the buildings
and the food and the people who shopped in 2014
are no longer on that part of the film.

Rinaldo Baker Machine

Rinaldo baker machine missing thirteen
nectar cogs, wrapped in Dracula cloaks,
ripped from swaths of star-dappled
Iranian night skies, advances towards
the sugary mammoth bread with a
Medieval icicle sword. "Not to worry,"
whispered the wooden magician, "Larry
gets off at midnight and we will
all go for muddy sin sandwiches
in his cab."

Maple Squares

Maple squares aroused the fish-handle
toolbox, spreading Chinese throat
nectar all over the luscious red steel
cabinet.

Who are you to question the integrity of
my collection of miniature crucified dogs?

Rented Box Lore

Rented box lore.
Dented face mixture.
In a tent, with you?!
Flattened propeller nonsense.
Incense patterned after Patton.
Mother in a juicy leprous apron.
Let's test the mentor
who rented dents.
Someone is going to pay for this.
And a kiss, with a rose,
with the hope that you will
take off your clothes.

Owl Boat

Owl Boat sucks out the moonlight
on a cruise to salt crust
lobotomy table.

Limousine lantern fable recited
over *Melies'* candle movies in an
opossum ice cube tray.

Roast Beef Lotion

Roast beef lotion lecture the professor
is a wave made of parakeets afflicted
with *Downs Syndrome* their plumage
a mixed fruit jam symphony and as the
black note dots fly away into G minor
all of the Chinese launder mats in 1941
post notices stating that they are
not Japanese funny how ignorance
suffocates reality like a warehouse eyeball
melting thousands of pairs of reading
glasses in a mucous furnace.

Cryptic Cackling

Cryptic cackling of Coptic monks
turns the one-armed sailor into a
cigar store Indian. Now the leopard
shadow rudder of the schooner is unmanned.
With a gorgeous Riviera tan, a man
named Stan impersonates the only
magician in the world who can turn a
pancreas into a lute.

Lucy got lost in the chute.
Oh! You brute.
Looted shoulder pipes strangled Mr.
Cake on the lake.

Dante was an optimist.

Frenzy

Frenzy
of wildly scattering,
frightened birds,
becomes
a hail
of rose-tinted
spider bullets shot by a
firing squad.
During the retarded muscle's dream,
it seems like the two hundred yard dash.
The runners are the bullets and each one
hits the center of
a
nectar bulls eye. Sweetly splashed nymphs
are naked.

Sanction Puff Jars

Sanction puff jars are malted in
the melted junction of Sam's mind.
But he is behind his butt in a
rut of rinds so unkind. Wind-up
pine toys. Smooth

> wood! Such a sensual
> haptic joy of
beautifully carved things which
ring throughout the doubts of us
all. My pall is all the rage
> these days!
> Much a tension napkin
> in the quiet skin of the
> drum dream.

Forensic Taste Conscience

Forensic taste conscience held a
casting call for a documentary
on public health code
violations, focusing on the preparation of
red dwarf soup. There will always
be a special place in my sponge
cake calcifuges for mentally challenged
preying mantis concertos. Viola
made some stink drinks. She
has a nice corpse. Coarse drapes
against the nape of my neck.

There May Have Been

There may have been a mouse in
the garage on the morning of the
St. Valentine's Day Massacre. The
poor little fellow must have been
severely traumatized by all of the
blood and bullet-ridden bodies. He
should have gotten a good lawyer
and sued Al Capone for pain and
suffering. Maybe it was better to have kept his mouth
shut. He probably would have gotten rubbed out
for being a rat.

Flesh Rash

Flesh rash, I was having dinner
with Bobby Darin. An alligator
suitcase surgeon tried to remove
Mack's knife from the back
of Mr. Darin's head. A nutmeg
sturgeon fought the shark (but the
shark bites).

Let's Get Lost

Let's get lost in the black
marble forest. There are sea
weed bow ties near the owl's
tree hole. He is made of
sparkling pirate ocean water.
Wherever he goes, he leaves a trail
of gold coins, 1920s
toasters, leather gangplanks,
mink eye patches, hallucinatory
robust magnetic jellied stench
derbies, idealistic dribbling hateful
pâté Pathe pavilion pavement,
and, of course, salty-tongued
parrots.

There Are Four Men in My Dream

There are four men in my dream.
They are wearing vintage deep sea
outfits, like *Diver Dan*.
A cup of coffee thinks it's
Halloween.
It floats by in a tuna costume.
One of the men pours in some
cream and sugar.
I awake and drink the coffee.
Around eleven a.m. I chew
some gum to get the fishy taste
out of my mouth.

Wyoming Ted

Wyoming Ted is a retired
tried and true Chinese bullfighter.
And there is a silver World War II
Zippo lighter on his Knighted
tiger maple night table. You must be
ready willing and able to board
the moribund rocket ship. Hooray
for the flutes made of smoke
because the joke is on the jury.

Utensils and Pencils

Utensils and pencils argued before
The Supreme Court.

Something about the difference
between design and utility.

Miners without fertility felt
guilty about the canaries but
a fork flung itself into
the Chief Justice's gavel.

It may take an extra effort
to unravel the decisions of
the court.

An Ice Cube Turned Fascist

An ice cube turned Fascist
objected to the brown shirt
aesthetics of *Mussolini*'s
1930s Italy. Pole-vaulting
assassins, using pre-*JFK*
Manlicher-Carcanos, took
practice shots at the freezer,
trying to influence the cube
by threatening his family.
Palermo patriots paused and the
green-glazed clay pasta bowl wept.

Bluto with Soppresseta Slices

Bluto with Soppresseta slices
for eyes
appears like a hologram in a
scene from *The Big Sleep*.
"That's three *Geiger*!" but
Popeye's nemesis stops the
bullet with his big beard.

Bogey is impressed and offers
him a *Camel*.

Olive tells *Lauren* that it's
OK to be called *Slim*.

No hard feelings.

Rippling Dark Wavelets

Rippling dark wavelets of
lusty *Merlot* are the
elegant purplish-black sky
lost in a dream of a
quaint Italian restaurant
on *Carmine* Street in
1940 where the red and
white checkered squares
of the table-cloth shiver
because the veal saltimbucca
is in love with a Russian
astronaut's *Mouse Trap* game
and *Big Jim Colosimo* is
supposed to get shot tonight.

Blue Vase Butter

Blue vase butter on the
graham cracker shutters
dusted daintily by the
effeminate butler who
likes to wear white silk
gloves while the master of
the house listens to Decca
78s with red labels and
there is a chilled bottle
of Don Perignon on the
table. Later in the stable
the master will do it faster
to the butler. Shudder! Shudder!

Cobweb Movie Screen

Cobweb movie screen in
a duel
at twenty paces
with
an anteater in a French horn
forest filled with
contaminated
tuxedo buttons.

Very elegant wooden pistol case.
Velvet indented
compartments
for the
weapons.

Creamy black.

There Is a Tortured Package

There is a tortured package of
midnight hidden somewhere in
1905 Coney Island.
It is a Bakelite radio conspiracy.
It is a basket of forlorn moose
injections.
All the clowns are in on it.
It is not a robot diary.
There are ghost sodas arguing with
cobwebs in the old rickety spook ride.

There Are a Series

There are a series of
triangular eggnog buttons
on the camp fire control
panel of the pig mischief
computer.

We were wed in a pewter
elevator.

Look at the 1950s constellations
reflected on teenage saliva
during all those first time
French kisses at the dance.

Placebo Timber Man

Placebo timber man
held akimbo
by redundant rescuers
who were furriers.
Johnny was mean to Barbara
in the 1968
Night of the Living Dead.
They're coming to get you.
A vet suit to there?
Zaire dents.
Lovely hue.

He Was Writing a Novella

He was writing a novella
about a sexually sardonic fella
who had rights to the bees
regardless of the macabre tease
of the girlie costumes in the hall.

That's all.

A Sorrento Bully

A Sorrento bully played a
Brillo cake pyramid.

Blue Formica 1950 kitchen
table having kidney trouble.

The black and white photography
in *Carnival of Souls*
is a soiled British trench coat
on a raw October afternoon.

Loose floorboards;
animal stink.
I want a drink.
Thor hoarding
walls.

Cannoli Cream Staircase

Cannoli cream staircase
tantalizes my foot. I am
walking naked over the
sugary steps and the dark
chocolate chips peep out of the
surface and tickle my toes.

Fountain Pen Nib

Fountain pen nib was
a sharpened scalpel in
the rambling nightmare
of a string quartet fleeing
the basement of the *Ho
Fat* Chop Suey joint circa
1946 at 42 *Mott* Street
because (you guessed it!) a
volcanic eyelid was sumptuously
defecating into a four foot
pewter stein and my mother
used to shop at *Klein*'s on
14th Street so nothing more
can be done for the ham radios
imbedded in the rectangular bars
of red soap.

During the Snow Fall

During the snow fall,
the flakes descend
in measured separation,
chalk stick
firemen circling their poles,
weeping cows
shedding milky crystal tears,
meshes of floating
white rope hoisted upon
ghost ships sinking in a
pale gauzy jumble.

Cantankerous Cannibals

Cantankerous
cannibals
convened during a curvaceous
caricature in miniature
mature
matador milestones
of lofty luscious
aloof soup.

A few Republicans have smeared
Hercules by inferring that he
performed oral sex on men
for money in a Texas
drive-in.

You don't say!

And *Elsa Lancaster* probably
never had to see *Charles Laughton*
naked because (mercifully) they had
what is called a marriage of
convenience.

Elsa was *Charlie's* beard.

No shit, *Sherlock*!

Quick Sand Memento Apron

Quick sand memento apron,
are you a pasteurized
Congo hat in a gorilla movie
of the "B" kind?

I will not engage in such
ruminations. Spidery thin
as angel hair pasta.
Clytemestra in a lime
green concertina boat.

You are trying to float into
my mischievous undulating out
of the way garage serenade.
I get paid one way or the other.

Mother of Messianic protuberances,
the swelling and the yelling are
symbiotic and rotten. *Joseph
Cotten* was hypnotic in
Journey into Fear.

A Ginger Snap Code Book

A ginger snap codebook
was playing *Clue* with some
vinegar-drenched salad armpits.

No more lead pipe. It was
probably the rope. But *Colonel
Mustard* doesn't like the library.

Esmerelda Mesmerized Zelda

Esmerelda
mesmerized
Zelda
with
her
velvet
vulva
while
a
ten
ton
tundra
under
the
Bonsai
sun
Ra
congratulated
Mr. Warbler
on
his
grape
tarantula.

You betcha!

There Could Be

There could be a noxious ferocity
in the rambunctious odious
lumps on the walls of the stalls
where the trenchant horses dream.

North of the abysmal monastery,
absinthe ordained, cleverly chiseled
stone penguins with dark blue breasts
pass the rest of us on the highway.

Someone packed the leather eyeglass
case with orange goose liver and
Samuel shivers when the gigantic
Bombay kettle quivers because the
Ganges rivers are dressed in fire-engine
red Zoot suits while admiring the
formality of the admiralty in the morning.

Variations

Copper snowmen with leprosy
arranged a warm iodine
feast in a plastic prison
for concrete dwarfs.

Coptic glow stems wilt Perry
caged alarms are fine at
least Ida's spastic pistons'
whore treats scarves.

Helicopter playpens bristle rosy
mélange a farm bovine
beast who was a sassy bison
lore of Lethe moths.

Crofter junkman with daisies
sustained no harm of mine
cease inner Nordic piston
for cold feet lofts.

Optic low stems wilt palsy
contagion a swarm of swine
peace Nirvana Aztec why son
horde peachy cloth?

Lop her Beekman Cherokee
and range a swarm of steins
cleats in a drastic wigwam
Zor replete forth.

Dapper choir hens with lunacy
avenged a worn magazine
crease in a haptic fist on
Thorazine neat larks.

Lapidary chores Ben's width Lucy
wedged acorn with Benzene
teasers Finland map stick wrist
orange jeans eat bark.

Rudimentary spores when girth juicy
hedges scorn Judith's dean
laser sins lap Nick mist
gleams of feet hark!

Nefertiti spare Glen dearth woozy
edges adjourn and pith so clean
bulldozer grin nap lick the gist
of beams beat Nick.

About the Author

PETER DELLOLIO was born in 1956 in New York City of first generation Italian-Americans. Went to Nazareth High School and New York University. Graduated 1978: B.A. Cinema Studies; B.F.A. Film Production. He has written and directed various short films, including James Joyce's short story "Counterparts," which he adapted into a screenplay. *Counterparts* was screened at national and international film festivals. As a freelance writer, he has published many articles and critical essays on the arts, including film, dance, sculpture, architecture and photography.

His poetry and fiction have appeared in numerous literary magazines, including *Antenna, Aero-Sun Times, Bogus Review, Pen-Dec Press, Both Sides Now, Cross Cultural Communications/ Bridging the Waters* and *The Mascara Literary Review*. His volume of one-act plays, *Habitual Rituals,* was published by Dramatika Press in 1983. One of the plays, "The Seeker," appeared in a 1998 issue of *Collages & Bricolages.*

Dellolio has been a contributing editor for *NYArts Magazine,* writing art and film reviews. He authored monographs on several new artists as well. He was co-publisher and editor-in-chief of *Artscape2000,* an award-winning art review e-zine. He has taught poetry and art for the LeAP expanded arts program in New York City. His paintings and 3D works are represented online.

His current long-term project is a critical study of Alfred Hitchcock, *Hitchcock's Cinematic World: Shocks of Perception and the Collapse of the Rational.* Excerpts have appeared in *The Midwest Quarterly, Literature/Film Quarterly, Kinema, Flickhead,* and *North Dakota Quarterly.*

He lives in Brooklyn, New York.

SELECTED ONLINE PUBLICATIONS

"Ineluctabilis," a short story in *The Mascara Review* No. 6, November 2009: mascarareview.com/peter-j-dellolio/

"Olive Oil in My Era: 50 Years of Evolution," an article in *The Olive Oil Times*, February 2014: http://peterdellolio.writersresidence. com/samples/olive-oil-in-my-generation-50-years-of-evolution

"Mars: Our Vanished Alter Ego?" and a painting series for the anniversary of JFK's assassination in *Democracy Chronicles*, October 2014: https://democracychronicles.com/author/peter-j-dellolio/

Art site: www.peterdellolio.com/

Other Xenos–Chelsea Collaborations

Available from Amazon.com
and Small Press Distribution: spdbooks.org

Claudia Zironi, *Eros and Polis: of that time when I was God in my belly.* Claudia Zironi turns the tables on male writers with her poetic reminiscences of former boyfriends and lovers. Her tone by turns is bemused, angry, grateful and sometimes revelatory. Her style is sharp, spare and paradoxical. ISBN 978-1-879378-99-5. Italian-English, 143 pages, $15.

Michael Palma, *Faithful In My Fashion: Essays on the Translation of Poetry.* Michael Palma, one of the outstanding translators of Dante in our time, discusses the art of translation and literary companionship in eleven genial and witty essays, plus an interview. ISBN 978-1-879378-99-5. English text, 93 pages, $10.

John Taylor, *The Dark Brightness.* An exploration of unfamiliar terrain, quiet and sensitive, with the senses heightened. The mood is enhanced by black and white graphics produced by three French artists – Sibylle Baltzer, Nelly Buret and Caroline Francois-Rubino – and one Greek – Dimitris Souliotis. ISBN 978-1-879378-84-1. English text, 86 pages, $10.

Alfredo de Palchi, *Nihil.* A challenging book of poetry and prose in which the author imaginatively floats down the river of his youth, the Adige, describes scenes of beauty and horror, and comments upon them. Each section of *Nihil* leads to more remote reaches of human experience and understanding. Translated, with a preface, by John Taylor. ISBN 978-1-879378-64-3. Italian-English, 183 pages, $15.

Elisa Biagini, *The Plant of Dreaming: Poems.* The author is known for her six books of poetry in Italy and for her prize-winning bilingual collection, *The Guest in the Wood* (Chelsea Editions, 2013). Her striving is to rediscover the reality in each moment, to capture the purity and pain of each experience. In *The Plant of Dreaming*, making further explorations, she enters into a creative dialogue with Paul Celan and Emily Dickinson. ISBN 978-1-879378-96-4. Italian-English, 205 pages, $15.